THE 80/20 MAKEOVER

THE 80/20 MAKEOVER

SUE DONNELLY

LEANMARKETING™
★PRESS★

First Published In Great Britain 2005
by Lean Marketing Press
www.BookShaker.com

Typeset in Georgia

To Cyndy.

Who always looks
absolutely fabulous.

Enjoy.

Sue
xx

Contents

Foreword

If you would like to learn the secrets of how to look just that bit better than Nature intended, The 80/20 Makeover is for you. Here you have instant access to the expertise of a highly–skilled Colour and Style Consultant in a book which is concise, clear, and very easy–to–read.

Is there anyone who wouldn't like to learn how to disguise their figure problems, look taller and slimmer, have a wardrobe that actually works and save time and money in the process? The benefits are not just for this season they stay with you forever.

During my ten years as a leading UK Image Consultant, I have advised thousands of people and read every book ever published on colour, style and image. What I love about The 80/20 Makeover is that it feels like a friend taking you through a fascinating personal process in a very easy–to–understand way. Sue shares her own concerns about her figure problems, and helps you with yours. Whatever your size or shape, this book offers practical solutions.

You will admire Sue's frankness and openness. I laughed out loud at her candid description of how her bottom was a figure problem. Then, when she reveals how she turns this liability into an asset by simply choosing a different jacket, you feel like cheering! You will say 'clever', 'simple' and 'yes, I could do the same'.

The 80/20 Makeover is the perfect little companion for anyone who dreams of a wardrobe of clothes that they can actually wear, and feel great in.

Jennifer Aston
www.aston–hayes.com
team@aston–hayes.com

Introduction

I've always been one of those people that regularly look in my overcrowded wardrobe and still find that I have nothing to wear. I'm pretty sure that the vast majority of us (female readers anyway) would wholeheartedly concur. Why is it that we can shop 'til we drop, yet nothing seems appropriate for the occasion?

Don't get me wrong, I am a big advocate of retail therapy and love nothing more than giving my well earned money to my favourite shops. However, there must be something not quite right if my wardrobe isn't working for me.

In 1906, Italian economist Vilfredo Pareto noticed that twenty percent of the people owned eighty percent of the wealth. He created a mathematical formula to describe this unequal distribution. Pareto's Principle, twenty percent of your effort achieves eighty percent of your results, was borne out of this fact and is used extensively in the business world.

Believe it or not, the same principle can apply to your wardrobe. If your wardrobe looks anything like mine, I'd place a bet that you wear twenty percent of your clothes, eighty percent of the time. While it's always great to have choice, think how much that eighty percent is costing you. Some people, mentioning no names, have been known to buy the same item twice or when searching for something to wear, have found an article they'd forgotten they'd bought!

To help you resolve this issue, I've created this book. It contains hints and tips so you will never again "have nothing to wear". It will help you identify your style, the clothes that best suit you, how to dress for success and how to spend your money wisely.

My clients have found, that although they own fewer items, they are able to create more outfits. In other words, a flexible, capsule wardrobe that works.

Enjoy!

Sue Donnelly, Jan 2005

The Body Beautiful

HOW TO MAKE THE MOST OF YOUR ASSETS

"Know first who you are and adorn yourself accordingly"
– Epicetus, Greek Philosopher

How many times have you spotted a fabulous garment in a shop window and gasped with delight? You've tried it on, taken it home, but it remains in the wardrobe because it doesn't look quite right somehow.

I know I've done it countless times. For me, it's usually when I'm trying to look feminine or when there's a big event coming up like a wedding or a party. The garment in question is usually something floaty and romantic and I ache to look good in it. But I don't.

As with everything, there is a good, scientific reason for this.

Think about Christmas and the time you spend wrapping all those presents. I don't know about you but I'm not too bad when the gift is a book or a box of some sort but as soon as I attempt to wrap something with curved edges I start having problems.

The same problem can also apply to "wrapping" our bodies. Trying to dress a curvy body in a stiff, starchy fabric is as difficult as wrapping a golf ball in an envelope. It won't fit properly unless lots of adjustments are made. Even the most expensive paper will not enhance the shape of the object. Furthermore, the package tends to look bigger and shoddily wrapped, however hard you've tried.

Conversely, a straight, angular object, like a ruler, does not fit well inside a flimsy wrapping. The corners poke through and the wrapping easily slips.

I'm not suggesting any of us is completely rotund or as straight as a stick but all of us lean more towards one shape than the other.

Looking at your body in an objective way and understanding your unique shape will determine how you can dress it in a way that will always look fantastic. Looking good and feeling great are inextricably linked. Understanding your assets and being able to capitalise on them will provide you with the means to create your own personal style. Neither contoured (round) or angular (straight) is the best option. Both can look terrific if you understand some of the style principles and use them accordingly.

CONTOURED OR ANGULAR?

Women

- Take a good look in a full length mirror, preferably in your undies.

- Work from the shoulders and down to your waist area.

- Do your shoulders slope or are they straight?

- Are your upper arms and shoulders softly padded or are they quite bony?

- Is your waist defined with hips that flare or not?

- Turn to the side view.

- Is your bust larger than a D cup or smaller?

- Does the small of your back curve in or is it straight?

If you answered Yes to the first part of the above questions, your upper body is contoured. If you answered Yes to the second part, then it is angular.

- Let's look at your bottom half

- Turn to the front view.

- Do you have definite hips that curve or are they "boyish"?

- Do you have a curve around the "saddle bag" area or are your legs straight?

- Turn again to the side.

- Is your bottom rounded or flattish?

- Do you have a tum or not?

If you answered mainly Yes the first part of the above questions then your lower body is contoured. If you answered mainly Yes to the second part, it's angular.

It is possible to have a different bodyline for the upper and lower halves of your body.

Men

- Take a good look in a full length mirror, preferably in your underwear.

- Look at the line of your shoulders compared to your hips and waist.

- If you have wide shoulders and small hips and waist, like an inverted triangle, you have an angular shape.

- Are your shoulders, waist and hips about the same width? If you tend towards portliness or have a bit of a tum, you are contoured. If you are lean with no spare flesh, think angular.

- If you have a comparatively wide waist or a large tum, then your overall shape is contoured. You may also have sloping shoulders.

The shape of your body determines the types of fabric that will suit it best. This includes its cut and also the patterns and finishes you should use.

In my case, the flimsy materials that I tried to wear to look feminine were too lightweight for my angular frame. Bones I didn't even know I had poked through the fabric, the straps kept falling down my shoulders, my bust became non–existent (this is bad news) and I looked, and felt, really uncomfortable. This is not how you want to feel when attending an important event. My attempt to look more romantic revolved around emulating the success of curvier women to achieve this look rather than dressing to enhance my own uniqueness.

Think also of someone like Jordan (Katy Price). Try and picture her trying to fit into a stiff cotton shirt. She may pull it off because of who she is, but for most of us, it just doesn't work. The fabric will strain against the body so the wearer looks uncomfortable and tortured. The same effect as wearing a strait–jacket.

So here are some guidelines to help you dress your body so that you'll always look and feel fabulous.

Fabrics...

Rounder (contoured) bodies look best dressed in soft fabrics that drape and skim. The fabric should be able to move with you rather than constrict. It should enhance your curves rather than squash or flatten. A fabric that skims will also slim the body.

Straighter (angular) bodies suit stiff, starchy fabrics. This applies to all items of clothing including jeans (lycra is a better bet for contoured bodies as it smooths over the curves).

Patterns...

Patterns and designs look great if they reflect your overall bodyline. Stripes, checks and other geometric shapes enhance the lines of an angular body. Abstract patterns, curves, spots, paisley and florals suit a contoured shape. Everyone can wear plain fabrics.

Cut...

The cut and finish of a garment can really enhance your natural shape. Look for straight seams, sharp or pointed lapels, slash pockets and straight hems if you are angular. A softer, more rounded cut is better suited to those with curves. Look for details such as softer lapels, rounded hems and pockets with curved flaps.

80/20 EXERCISE

Let's start putting our 80/20 Principle into action.

You now have a clear idea of your bodyline
and what best suits you.

Take some time to go through your wardrobe.

Look at garments that you haven't worn for a while.
Do they follow the principles set out above?
If not, let some nice charity benefit.

Size Is Everything

GETTING THE BALANCE RIGHT

*"I love to go shopping. I love to freak out salespeople.
They ask me if they can help me, and I say, 'Have you got
anything I'd like?' Then they ask me what size I need,
and I say, 'Extra medium.'"*
– Steven Wright

They say size isn't important but, in fact, where style is concerned, it is. The patterns you wear, the weight of the fabric, your accessories, even your heel height will look considerably better if the size reflects that of your body. If these things don't reflect your size then you're in danger of looking eccentric, over–powering or lost.

Think about Dame Edna Everage. Probably not an icon you'd wish to emulate but she does demonstrate the point. Everything she wears, from her over sized specs, to the glittery costumes and the "big" hair yell bad taste. But some of us do this on a regular basis without even being aware of it.

Look at the diagram below:

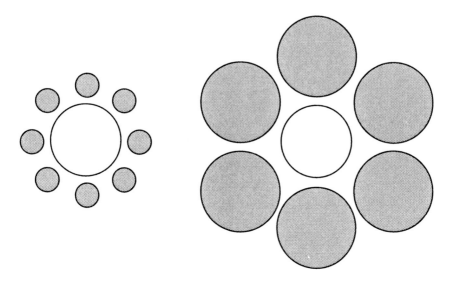

Which of the inner circles looks the smaller?

Actually the circles are the same size. The one surrounded by the larger circles only appears to be smaller because it is overshadowed by the larger ones.

If you wear clothes or patterns that are too large for you, you will appear swamped. Unfortunately, you will not look smaller, so if you're larger than you'd like to be, it's not an easy get out clause to exercise or eating sensibly! Conversely, if you wear too small a scale, you will look much bigger. While this may be okay for some guys, I can't imagine many ladies thinking likewise.

You'll be pleased to know that scale is relative to bone structure and not to the amount of fat you carry. So ladies, when I ask you to find a tape measure, hopefully, you'll not have a heart attack.

HOW TO FIND YOUR SCALE

Women

Take the tape measure and measure around your wrist.

If your wrist measures:

- Under 5½ inches/ 14 cm – you're small scale

- 5½ – 6½ inches/ 14–16cm – medium

- Over 6½ inches/ 16cm – large

Height is also a consideration but it is possible to be a tall person (over 5ft 6") and have a small scale or be short (under 5ft 3") and have large scale.

Men

I'm guessing that most of you won't bother taking your wrist measurement, so let's go on height and build as the main criteria.

Cross reference the following chart to work out your scale.

	LIGHT	AVERAGE	HEAVY
> 5 ft 11"	MEDIUM	LARGE	LARGE
5 ft 7" – 5 ft 11"	LIGHT	MEDIUM	LARGE
< 5 ft 7"	SMALL	SMALL	MEDIUM

In the previous chapter, I mentioned my longing to look feminine and how the fabric of my floaty outfit didn't suit my angular body. There was another reason why it didn't look great. The scale was wrong. As someone who is medium scale, the weight of the chiffon was too light.

To get an idea of scale worn badly, imagine a large scale lady spilling over the edge of her small, kitten heels or a very tiny girl wearing huge, platform soles.

One of my male clients always carried a briefcase that was huge. He may have felt powerful when it was in his possession but the perception to others was one of a small minded person hiding behind a prop. It was incongruent with his size and his stature.

Get the idea?

So here are guidelines for you to think about:

Small Scale

- Fabric weights should be light. Men, suiting weight about 10−12oz.

- Patterns should be small and also reflect your bodyline, for instance a small diamond patterned tie would look great on small scale, angular man.

- Accessories (apart from specs, which are covered in a later chapter, should reflect both your scale and your bodyline). A small, floppy handbag will look fantastic on a small scale contoured woman.

- Ladies, shoes should have a small, neat heel.

Medium Scale

- Fabric should be of medium weight. Men, suiting weight about 12oz.

- Patterns should be medium size and reflect your bodyline, for instance a medium paisley print tie would look great on you if you have a contoured body. Choose medium size checks or stripes if you're angular.

- Accessories (apart from specs, which are covered in a later chapter) should reflect both your scale and your bodyline. A medium size, stiff leather handbag will look fantastic on a medium scale, angular woman. If you're contoured, opt for a fabric that moves, such as suede or fabric.

- Ladies, shoes should have a medium heel. If you want to add drama, you can choose stiletto or platform as long as the rest of your outfit is in scale.

Large Scale

- Fabrics should be the heaviest weights. Men, suiting weight about 12–14oz.

- Patterns should be large and also reflect your bodyline, for instance a large check tie would look great on a large scale, angular man. Opt for large swirls or paisleys if you're contoured.

- Accessories (apart from specs, which are covered in a later chapter) should reflect both your scale and your bodyline. A large handbag will look fantastic on a large scale woman. Choose stiff leather if you're angular and a softer leather if you're contoured.

- Ladies, shoes should have a chunky heel. If you wish, you can go for height, depends on how tall you want to look.

What Have You Learned?

My scale is

....

Fabric weight is

....

Patterns are

....

....

....

....

Accessories

....

....

....

....

Drama can be created by up–scaling. A large piece of jewellery (including a watch), a higher heel, or a bolder pattern can all get you noticed. ONE area only though or you'll end up looking like Dame Edna!

A word about accessories. Some people think that you should always buy the best quality fabrics you can afford when purchasing your clothes. These days, it seems that people are in two camps: those who buy designer labels and bespoke tailoring and those who prefer the "throw away" culture of cheaper items. With top names designing for high street stores (for instance Jasper Conran and Ben De Lisi for Debenhams, Karl Lagerfeld for H&M) you can achieve a stylish look at a great price. The let down is always with the accessories. Unless you're looking for a "fun" look, choose accessories that are classic and show quality and good taste. At interviews, for instance, you can bet money on the fact that your shoes, bag/briefcase, watch, jewellery and pen will be noticed.

80/20 EXERCISE

Here's your 2nd action to help clear out the 80% of your wardrobe rarely worn.

Look at the designs and fabrics of your clothes. Are some too heavy? If so, they will add bulk. Are some too light? They'll probably make you look bigger.

Check out your ties, guys. If you're angular, throw out the ones with contoured designs and vice versa if you have a contoured shape. Check out the size of the pattern you're wearing. Is it too large or too small?

Are your handbags too large, small, stiff or floppy? Unless you absolutely cannot bear to part with an item (sentimental reasons mainly), get rid of it now. I expect you'll find the items you discard are the ones that never looked or felt quite right anyway.

Look at your jewellery. Does it look cheap? Is it dated? If so, dump it. There's something really cleansing about throwing out the old to make way for the new.

It's All An Illusion

THE ART OF CHEATING

"Illusion – the sensuous perception of an external object involving a false belief"
– Oxford English Dictionary

Unfortunately, most of us do not look like Kate Moss or David Beckham, with or without clothes. However, all is not lost. This chapter is about cheating, and is the only part of the book dedicated to making you into something you're not!

Apart from being beautiful, models have something else – Perfect Proportions:

- shoulders wider than hips
- long waist
- long legs

As long as we can create the illusion of having these proportions in our own bodies, we too can look model–like.

It's all about lines. Those of you with an interest in art, architecture or maybe geometry will know there are 4 types:

1. Vertical – runs up and down

2. Horizontal – runs side to side

3. Diverging/Converging – creates a V. Diverging at the widest points, converging where they meet at the narrowest point.

4. Diagonal – from top to bottom, left to right or vice versa.

Our natural shape can be altered by using these lines so that a different image is perceived by the viewer:

- Vertical lines create length.

- Horizontal and diverging lines create width

- Converging lines will narrow.

- Diagonal lines – depends on the angle. The more vertical, the more length is created, the more horizontal, the more shortening.

- Clever use of lines can make short legs appear longer, small busts look larger, shoulders look wider and so on.

UNDERSTANDING YOUR PROPORTIONS

The first thing to do is to understand your own proportions. You may need a friend to help you.

To check whether your legs are short or long...

- Take off your shoes.

- Take a tape measure and measure the distance from your groin to the floor.

- Now measure from the same place to the top of your head.

- If the first measurement is smaller, you have short legs in proportion to your height.

- If it's longer, you have longer legs.

Don't get hung up on the fact that you have to buy longer (or shorter) length trousers. This exercise is about the proportion between one body area and another, and not actual length.

Your waist...

- It's not the measurement around the girth but the length of the waist that is important.

- Ladies, place your tape measure under your bust at the centre of your breastbone.

- Measure the distance between this point and your natural waist indent.

- If it's less than 3 inches, you are short waisted.

- Gents, generally speaking, if you have short legs you are long waisted and vice versa. This often applies to naturally large breasted women too. Lucky you – large boobs and long legs!

Your shoulders...

- Stand in front of a mirror and check whether the edges of your shoulders are wider or narrower than your hips at the widest point.

- If unsure, ask a friend to check from the back view.

What Have You Learned?

My proportions are

1. Legs

....

1. Waist

....

1. Shoulders

....

I am one of those people who at 5ft 4" have a very long body and really short legs. Delegates are amazed when I impart this fact at my workshops. They believe I am taller than my actual height and have legs that go on forever. I use my knowledge to change what I haven't got naturally into something I'd love to have. Who cares if it's cheating?

Here's how it can work for you:

Short Legs...

- Need vertical lines to create length.

- Avoid turnups on trousers as the horizontal line will shorten the leg. This also applies to tapered trousers. Make sure they are long enough. Men's should break on the shoe. Ladies, yours should touch where your toes crease.

- Boot leg cut is very flattering for shorter legs.

- Vertical stripes or a centre crease give the illusion of length.

- Shorter skirts (knee length) are more flattering than long ones. Wear with knee high boots that touch the hem of the skirt or coordinating tights. Any gap will shorten the leg. Asymmetric hems are also a good idea as they divert attention away.

- Pointed toe shoes will lengthen, rounded will shorten as will any horizontal bars in the design. Avoid ankle straps at all costs. Try flip flop V design rather than sliders in the summer.

- Heels make legs look longer.

- Jackets should be no longer than bum length. Shorter jackets look good as long as you have no challenges round the hip or tum area.

- Belts should match bottoms rather than tops.

Short Waist...

- Needs vertical lines to create length.

- Avoid any horizontal lines on your top half as they will widen and make you look fatter. Vertical lines will slim.

- Drop waisted or hipster trousers give length to your upper body.

- Single breasted jackets and cardigans flatter whilst double breasted will give the illusion of width. Keep the jacket open if you want to appear slimmer.

- Trousers and skirts without waistbands. Guys, wear braces for a funky look especially if you are large around your girth. If you do wear a belt, match it to your top half not the bottom.

- Wear shirts and tops worn out rather than tucked in.

- Longer skirts and jacket lengths look good.

- Simple unstructured clothing rather than fitted will look better on you.

Narrow Shoulders...

- Need horizontal or diverging lines to create width.

- Wide lapels and shirt collars give the illusion of width.

- Avoid halter necks as all eyes will be on your boobs! Also avoid raglan, three quarter, or sleeveless garments.

- Trench Coats with detail on the shoulder.

- Sleeves with widening lines such as capped, petal, dolman or ruched.

- Off the shoulder styles – women only! Or try wrapping a scarf or pashmina round your shoulders.

- Shoulder pads (as long as they are fashionable or part of your suit tailoring).

- Avoid excessive pleating or bulk around the hips as this will also make your shoulders look out of proportion.

The use of colour can also help distract. Bright or light colours in shiny fabrics will draw attention whilst dark colours in a matt fabric will deflect.

80/20 EXERCISE

Your task is to now go and look again at your wardrobe. Which clothes aren't doing you any favours in the "model" department? Cast them aside.

You want to look fabulous don't you?

Rise To The Occasion

AND OTHER (FIGURE) CHALLENGES

"Do not strive for immortality but make the most of the possibilities that are open to you"
– Old Indian Proverb

Now we've all got long legs, wide shoulders and newly acquired model looks, what else could we wish for? I know from experience, my own and my clients', that we often have a problem with a certain area of our body. So much so, that we often fixate on it – even though other people rarely notice or cannot understand what we're worried about. If it's real for you, it won't make much difference what others say, it will still cause you concern.

I have a very low slung bum due to my very long back. From the front I look OK but from the back I always feel my bum is drooping further and further towards my knees. You may not notice this but I do – and this is what counts.

I've now developed a look that completely hides my bum, still gives me a great outline and always looks stylish. A fitted jacket, with a knee length hem, can be worn over jeans, trousers and a skirt. You cannot tell where my bum is and the rest of my body looks great. This type of jacket also works well to disguise saddle–bags.

Wearing a wraparound cardigan and tying a large bow at the back also takes the attention away from my bum. It's a question of finding out what works for you and using it to your advantage.

If you have no problems with any part of your body, you can skip the rest of this chapter and move onto the next one. If, like most of us, you do – keep reading.

LADIES

Disguising a Full Bust...

Women with large boobs often have a short neck. An opening at the neck, such as a V neck or a scoop, will break up the area. Try open neck shirts, or a crossover V sweater is particularly flattering. A closed neckline, for instance a polo neck or a poncho, will make the bust appear larger

- A full bust means a contoured outline, so stick to curved lines on top. Avoid details and prints that draw focus to the breasts, especially horizontal stripes or pockets.

31

- The correct bra is essential. It can take pounds off you. Don't wear lacy bras with T–shirts or close fitting fabrics.

- Dark colours in a matt fabric will draw attention from the bust area. Bright colours and shiny fabrics attract attention.

- Longer line jackets, with single breasted fastenings and long sleeves look great on large busts. Try wearing a scarf draped round the neck and falling over the chest area to create length.

- Ruching is great as you can't tell what is you and what is fabric. It hides a multitude of sins.

- Avoid halter neck tops, especially with unsupported boobs and sleeves ending at the bust line. Also avoid tops with sleeves ending at the bust line.

Enhancing a small bust...

Padded bras and "chicken fillets" are a must if you want to look like you have a cleavage. Aim for a smooth finish under clingier fabrics. Most stores sell T–shirt bras which do the job well.

- Wearing lots of thin layers can add bulk to the chest area without making you look fat.

- Polo necks look great on smaller chests.

- Ruching is good as you can't tell what is your chest and what is the fabric.

- Pockets, stripes and patterns placed on the bust area can enhance the chest size.

- Short sleeves ending at the bust line create a horizontal line creating width.

- Off the shoulder, halter neck, patterns and textures look great on a smaller chest.

- Light colours in shiny fabrics attract attention.

- Avoid necklines that are too low.

Disguising a pear shaped figure...

The focus needs to be drawn away from the bum and hips.

- Wear long jackets that don't cut across the hip line or your widest point.

- Dark colours on the bottom and lighter colours on your upper body will draw the attention away from your lower half.

- Jewellery and scarves are good diversionary tactics.

- Boot cut trousers/jeans, trousers without waistbands, and wearing fabrics that don't cling are a wise choice.

- Avoid too much detail around the waist such as belt loops or pleating.

Hiding a full tum...

To skim is to slim so dress to divert attention away from your mid section.

- Single breasted jackets and coats will lengthen and slim the body, especially if they are longer length.

- Wear the same colour on upper and lower body.

- Try dresses and tops with an empire line or no visible waistline.

- Avoid belts round the waist or things tucked in.

Building a secure foundation...

- Ladies – the wrong underwear can ruin an outfit instantly.

- Spend time and money on selecting the right size and style. It can instantly transform your shape and you will look pounds lighter.

- Bras in lacy fabrics worn under a T–shirt or a sheer blouse add lots of bulk so make sure you choose the correct style for your outfit.

- VPL (visible panty lines) are a real no–no. Larger tums or bums can benefit from knickers that "hold you in." whereas G strings are still useful for those with pert behinds. But make no mistake, Bridget Jones' big pants are definitely out!

MEN

Portly Tum...

- Dress to divert attention away from your mid section.

- Single breasted jackets and coats will lengthen and slim. Avoid double breasted as they will make you look fatter.

- Trousers need to fit properly around the waist, and that means your actual waist, not the low slung look many men go for. Pleating will provide comfort. If the waistband sits under your natural waist, try braces instead.

- Many men make the mistake of wearing their trousers too short. Trousers should break on the shoe and should be slightly longer at the back of the heel than at the front of the shoe.

- Avoid T–shirts which accentuate your tum and make it look larger. This also applies to any other garment that "hugs" you in the wrong place.

- A waistcoat, or a sleeveless sweater worn over your shirt can have a very slimming effect. Keep to a dark colour.

- Light coloured trousers can widen your hips so wear darker fabrics for a more flattering effect.

- Avoid ties that are too bold or too wide as they can draw attention to the mid section.

80/20 EXERCISE

Have another good look at your wardrobe.

Can you change the way you wear some of your clothes so that they become more flattering?

Re–read the guidelines above and use them to revamp what you have already.

Forget The Botox

LET THE RAINBOW HELP YOU

"Pink is not a colour, it's a state of mind"
– unknown

Forget the botox! Wearing the right colours can enhance your complexion far more than any makeup. And guys, this applies to you too!

You may be surprised to know that 1 in 7 men are colour blind and 1 in 4 cannot distinguish between shades and tones of a particular colour.

The current trend is for us to be "warmed up". Cosmetic counters offer bronzing powers and fake tans to turn us into golden beauties. Hairdressers often promote gold or copper highlights to provide a warm glow around our face. But "being warmed" doesn't actually suit all of us. In fact we can be in danger of looking jaundiced or sallow with colours that are too yellow for our natural complexion. And I'm guessing that no–one would choose to look ill?

For years I was a golden blonde. I never felt it was quite right but the hairdresser said it suited me and I went along with it. I applied stacks of makeup, bronzers and a really dark lipstick to balance out my look. Now I realise my instinct was correct. I am now a striking silver blonde. As it suits my colouring, I need less makeup, my eyes are brighter and I look younger than I did before. That's the magic of colour!

CHOOSING THE RIGHT COLOURS

You'll need a mirror for this exercise. It's also useful to have a friend with you as they can be more objective.

- To check which colours suit you best, hold fabrics that are individually dark, light, cool (blue/pink based) and warm (yellow based) against your face.

- Observe what happens to your skin.

- Some colours may cast shadows giving a "grey" look around the jaw or under the eyes.

- Warm colours on a cool skin may result in a jaundiced look.

- Bright colours will suit both men and women with bright eyes or contrasting complexion (think Snow White).

- Soft, muted colours will suit those with less contrast between hair, eyes and skin (think Cindy Crawford).

- Colours that are too bright can overwhelm and look garish – a good example of the clothes wearing you rather than the other way round.

- Shades that are too muted can give the face a wishy–washy appearance with no real definition to the features.

Write down what has happened and use this for the basis of selecting colours in the future. If you looked good in dark and bright colours, choose these, as soft and light colours probably will not suit you. If the warmer tones of yellow and cream suited you, odds are the cooler tones of blue and pink will be as flattering.

When buying makeup or having your hair coloured it is worth asking the consultant or hairdresser to assess your skin tone.

Professional hairstylists should be aware of the difference between cool and warm tones and be able to advise accordingly. There are many shades of blonde or red highlights for your hair. It's important to choose the one that suits both your complexion and your natural hair colour or you can look drained.

- **Cool Blonde (think Naomi Watts):** Ash, Pearl, Creamy Blonde or Beige (avoid gold or red).

- **Cool Redhead (think Nicole Kidman):** Peach and Strawberry Blonde.

- **Cool Brunette (think Lorraine Kelly):** Beige and Nut Brown (avoid gold or red).

- **Cool Black (think Beverley Knight):** Beige and Coffee hues, Aubergine and Pink.

- **Warm Blonde (think Cameron Diaz):** Gold, Champagne or Honey.

- **Warm Redhead (think Susan Sarandon):** Rich Russet and Copper.

- **Warm Brunette (think Jennifer Aniston):** Gold, Copper, Treacle.

- **Warm Black (think Beyonce):** Honey, Amber, Caramel and Toffee.

Selected cosmetic houses, such as Prescriptives, sell foundations in hundreds of shades to enable you to easily pick the one that perfectly matches your skin tone.

80/20 EXERCISE

Now you know the types of colours that suit you.
You have a choice.

You can discard clothes in shades that are not flattering or you can work out a way to wear them.

This may mean using a scarf or a tie in a flattering colour. As long as the colour does not sit right next to your skin, you can get away with it.

On the whole, we tend to buy colours that we like. Often this is instinctively because we know they look good.

Mirror, Mirror On The Wall

ADORE YOURSELF

"I think the most important thing a woman can have –
next to talent of course – is her hairdresser."
– Joan Crawford

Your face is probably the most important part of your body. It's often the first thing we notice about someone, whether in a business meeting or across a crowded room.

If you're like me, you'll probably only notice the "bad" bits. Your concentration will be on whether you have more wrinkles, bags under your eyes or spots. If you're like my husband, you'll probably never look in the mirror at all!

Understanding the shape of your face and your features will help you to look more authentic. This in turn will enhance your natural beauty and good looks. You'll be able to choose hairstyles, specs and jewellery that really do you justice. Guys – it will also affect how you wear your shirt and tie.

HOW DOES YOUR FACE SHAPE UP?

Using a mirror, look at your facial features.

- Is your nose long and straight or is it small, short or full?

- Do your eyebrows sit straight or are they arched?

- Are your eyes small or almond shaped or are they large and round?

- Do you have visible cheekbones and planes within your face or are your cheeks soft and plump?

- Are your lips thin and straight or plump and large?

- Is your chin square or angular or is it soft or rounded?

Keep your mirror handy as you'll need this later.

If you answered mainly "Yes" to the first answer in each of the questions, you have angular features.

If you answered mainly "Yes" to the second part of the answers, your features are contoured. You may remember we touched on these terms when looking at body shapes.

Don't worry if your facial features are different to your body shape. It is possible to have a body that is one shape and a face that is another.

If you have long hair, tie it back so that the outline of your face is visible. Starting at the top of your head, use both hands to trace the outline with your fingertips so you can really see its shape. Is it wide or long? Do you have a more pronounced jawline?

On the whole, people with angular features will have a square or rectangular face. Contoured features normally reside in an oval or round face.

We need to go back to the art of illusion again. If your face is very narrow, then it helps to make it appear wider. Conversely, if it's wide we need to lengthen it.

Long faces best suit hairstyles that provide some width. A high pony tail or lots of hair on top of the head will only add to the illusion of length, as will very long straight hair. Create balance by having more hair at the sides of your face or curling the hair out and way from the face. If your jaw is pointed, hair will look great if wide at this point as it will detract attention away.

- Spectacles and sunglasses should fit outside the contours of the face. This provides a horizontal line which shortens and widens.

- If you also have a long nose, choose plastic rather than metal frames. The thicker, dark bridge will shorten the nose.

- Avoid long dangly earrings as these will also drag the eye downwards. Look for earrings that are wide and sit at ear level.

- You can add width to longer faces by wearing a wider cutaway collar and a wider tie. Avoid long pointed collars as these will lengthen it even more.

Wide faces need to look longer, so hairstyles with height on the top or length at the bottom will achieve this. Square jaws can be complemented by longer styles and a side fringe. Avoid a jaw length bob and a straight fringe as this style can resemble a window frame with curtains.

- Spectacles should sit inside the contours of the face. A high bridge in metal will lengthen the nose if required.

- Earrings that are long and dangly, or hoops that appear long when viewed from the front will add required length to the face.

- Avoid wide ties and cutaway collars if your face is wide. Lengthen by using longer, pointed shirt collars and a narrower tie.

On the whole, general style principles apply just as they did to your body shape. If you have an angular face, think stiff fabrics around the neck, geometric shaped glasses and sharp haircuts. Contoured faces need more softness and look good with wavier hair, slightly curved frames and softer fabrics round the neck.

80/20 EXERCISE

Are you making the most of your biggest asset?

Do you need to change your hair, your specs or your shirts?

It can make a massive difference to your appearance

and once you've got it right, you'll positively

brim with confidence.

Who Are You?

FINDING THE REAL YOU

"The most exhausting thing you can be is inauthentic"
– Anne Morrow Lindbergh

Now we get down to the real nitty gritty. You've established your overall body and face shape, the colours that best suit you and how to disguise any figure challenges. Well done for getting this far.

This chapter is all about dressing in an authentic way. It's no good following the rules, if you don't feel comfortable with the overall result. Clothes should be an extension of your personality not a suit of armour or a mask.

I have a slim, angular body and the expertise to make my legs appear much longer than they are. In theory, I would look good wearing a short leather mini skirt, high heels and fishnet stockings. However, this style of dress does not fit in with my overall values. The result – I would look and feel uncomfortable, lose my confidence and probably bolt for the nearest hiding place. This is even more alarming when you understand that "talking" to people is one of my pleasures in life and I'm very well practised!

A client of mine works in an office environment where suits are the norm for both men and women. She is a larger than life, bubbly person and the idea of her in a buttoned up suit just does not sit well.

Between us, we've managed to create a look that fits in with her corporate lifestyle but also expresses her own unique personality.

Instead of using pin–stripes and severe tailoring in her clothing, she has selected a less structured style of suit. She wears this with brightly coloured blouses with frilly collars in soft fabrics. She looks professional, but liberated at the same time. Her hair is left loose or pinned back, with tendrils to soften her face. She looks fantastic and radiates confidence. Guess what?

She is also highly successful; because she looks and feels confident, she attracts colleagues and clients who want to work with her. All good news for the bottom line.

There are some items that scream out a message as soon as you see them. I'm thinking of "novelty" ties for example. While the owner may think they are fun to wear, I can assure you that the rest of us do not! So be authentic but also be aware of the environment in which you operate.

80/20 EXERCISE

1. Think about the words you would use to describe yourself. Make a list and group them so you are narrowing down to 2 or 3 key adjectives.

2. Look at your style of dress. Does it fully express the words you've just used about yourself? If not, why not?

3. What can you do to dress in a more authentic manner?

4. Ask someone you trust to describe you. Are their descriptors the same as yours? If not, ask them why they see you differently. Does your style have anything to do with it? Are your clothes giving the wrong impression?

5. Look again at the revised contents of your wardrobe. Do the garments you still own fit in perfectly with your lifestyle? For instance, if you spend 75% of your time at work, does your wardrobe reflect this? If it's full of track suits, you may want to ask why that is? Are you hiding your full potential?

As the Greek Philosopher, Epicetus once said "Know first who you are and then adorn yourself accordingly"

To Be Or Not To Be

DRESSING TO CHANGE YOUR APPROACH

"The key to the ability to change is a changeless sense of who you are, what you are about, and what you value."
– Stephen R Covey

There are times in our lives when we can become anxious or nervous. It might be a presentation to the board, a blind date, meeting your girlfriend's mother for the first time and so on. We could all do with a little help on these occasions, without hitting the gin bottle.

You may not be aware of it, but colour is a powerful medium when it comes to tackling everyday situations. You may even be wearing a colour which sends out a signal, albeit subconsciously. Pink, for instance, is thought to be the colour of love, so wearing it may be an attempt to surround ourselves with love or even attract love into our lives.

Think about situations that might cause anxiety in your life, or occasions when you need to be motivated. Using the following guide, discover how wearing a particular colour can help and assist you when you most need it. The colour does not have to apply to the entire outfit, sometimes just a splash will do the trick.

RED – Red has the longest wavelength, so we see it first (think traffic lights, brake lights and so on). It is stimulating and courageous. Wear it if you want to be noticed, powerful, assertive or strong.

ORANGE – A mixture of yellow and red symbolising passion, abundance and fun. Beware though, not many of us carry off this colour well. So wear as a complimentary or accent colour unless you want to look like you've be Tango'd!

YELLOW – An emotional colour that governs extraversion, friendliness, creativity and optimism. It represents our personal power and how we feel about ourselves. A spot of yellow can go along way to making you feel more confident.

GREEN – The least worn colour in the UK, perhaps because of its "unlucky" connotations. Green signifies balance, compassion and understanding. A useful colour to wear if you have a difficult client, a confrontation or an apology to make! Also useful to enable balance within if you feel "out of sorts".

BLUE – Governs speech, communication, creative expression and intellect. Wear it when presenting a speech or if you need a clear thought pattern. A serene and soothing colour, it mentally calms.

VIOLET – A spiritual colour that is also thought to represent authenticity, truth and luxury (Cadbury's Dairy Milk was perceived to be very expensive chocolate due to its purple wrapper).

PINK – Love and femininity. We all have a feminine side. So men, you can still wear pink with pride. A soothing colour which radiates warmth and love.

BROWN – Earthy and reliable, though can be construed as dull. It's warmer and softer than black and can look more flattering on warmer skins.

BLACK – Everyone's favourite "safe" bet. Exudes sophistication, glamour, efficiency, and security. Often worn as a slimming aid (though this does not work for everyone) it can drain and become serious. Wear with caution unless you know it suits you.

WHITE – White is a total reflection and represents purity. Can be perceived as hygienic and sterile which is why it's used in hospitals and clinics worldwide.

GREY – A neutral colour. Grey can have a dampening effect on other colours and can indicate a lack of confidence.

Your clothes can also have an effect when you need to modify your behaviour to get the best result.

YOUR PERSONALITY

I'd like you to think about your own personality.

- Where would you sit on a scale of 1 – 10 with shy at 1 and aggressive at 10?

- Are there certain circumstances when it would be beneficial to move up or down the scale to appear more authoritative or less demanding?

- The way you put your clothes together can help you to achieve this.

One of my clients is a manager of a sales team. He is expected to get great results and, on the whole, he achieves this. However, he realised that many of the team seemed to be in awe of him and rarely did any of them call him for help. Even during team meetings he felt that he was doing all the talking and the input from his team was minimal.

We looked at his style of dress. He was wearing a charcoal grey, well–tailored suit, white crisp cotton shirt and a deep red tie. He looked fabulous BUT without knowing it, his adopted style was that of an authoritarian.

I suggested he tone down the colours so there would be less contrast between them. A paler grey suit with blue shirt and blue tie, for instance. He still looked like a smart businessman BUT he appeared to be more approachable. The result? His staff opened up more to him as they felt less intimidated.

Here are some tips that will help you to adapt and connect more effectively with people:

1. Authority is gained by wearing clothes with maximum contrast: black and white, dark brown and cream, navy and palest blue.

2. A softer image is gained by dressing in tones and shades of a single colour: olive green trousers/skirt and slightly lighter shade for the upper body.

3. Plain, bold colour is authoritative.

4. Introduce pattern or design for a softer look, for instance a paisley tie with a striped shirt.

5. The larger the stripe or check in a shirt or blouse, the more casual it appears.

6. A jacket that compliments, but doesn't exactly match, trousers or a skirt will appear less authoritative.

7. Fabrics that are stiff and starchy will appear more authoritative than those that have more fluidity and drape. The same applies to garments with lots of fitted tailoring (authority) and less structure (approachable).

8. Red and/or black can look powerful. Pastels will appear less so.

9. Guys – a button down collar in a softer fabric will look less authoritative than a stiff cutaway.

10. Hairstyles that are severe will give an impression of power. Hair softly framing the face alludes to warmth.

80/20 EXERCISE

How can you build these tips into your wardrobe and your everyday life?

Pareto Is In Your Wardrobe

YOUR OWN STYLE AT A GLANCE

"Fine feathers make fine birds"
– Proverbs

By now you should have sorted out the old, the dated and the inappropriate clothes from your wardrobe. You should be left with less garments but a wider choice of outfits that will see the light of day.

To celebrate why not apply what you've learned and do a little enlightened shopping? This time, I'm confident you'll buy clothes that you'll wear regularly and that will give you an edge.

To keep the 80/20 rule working for you take a leaf out of the chic Parisienne's book. These french women always look stylish because they plan their wardrobe and their shopping. So instead of buying individual garments on a whim, think about what they will complement in your existing collection. As a rule of thumb, if it doesn't go with three other items, don't buy it.

To manage your new collection and to make it easier to combine your existing garments, hang clothes by type. Put your jackets together, your trousers, shirts and so on. That way you can spot different combinations more easily. If you prefer, you can also differentiate by colour. Do the same for your boots, shoes and sandals. This should save you time when dressing.

You'll now look fantastic, feel more confident, have money in the bank and of course, never again will you have nothing to wear!

Summary

ALL ABOUT YOU

My Body Line is

....

Fabrics I can wear are

....

....

The Best Cut is

....

Patterns

....

....

....

My Scale is

....

Accessories

....

....

....

....

My Proportions are

1. Legs

....

2. Waist

....

3. Shoulders

....

To create an illusion of _____ I need to wear

....

....

....

My figure challenges are

....

....

....

To disguise them I need to

....

....

....

My Face Shape is

....

The best hairstyle for me is

....

Specs and sunglasses should be

....

Collars

....

My 3 adjectives are

1. ....

2. ....

3. ....

Accentuate – the accent on U, your image and your impact.

Sue Donnelly is an Image Coach with a wide experience of working with people both in a corporate environment and on a personal basis. She has held a variety of senior management positions for Thomas Cook, Citibank and Insights Learning & Development where image was a crucial factor in attracting and retaining business partnerships. Sue's work with individuals enables them to find a style of dress that reflects their inner values and unique personality, elevating self–esteem and confidence. Corporate work includes personal branding, personal effectiveness, seminars and workshops. Her work has been featured in national magazines and newspapers and she has been invited to appear on prime time TV. She is also the resident style expert for www.expertsonline.tv. A qualified life coach, fitness instructor and workshop facilitator, Sue has a passion for helping both men and women to look and feel good about themselves in an authentic way, whatever their age, shape or size.

For more information or to book a private session:
Phone 0845 123 5107,
Email: *accentuate@fsmail.net*
Website: *www.thebigu.com*

NOTES

NOTES

Printed in the United Kingdom
by Lightning Source UK Ltd.
104090UKS00001B/163-219